Contents

Amy's first years

This is Mr William Johnson and his wife Amy. About 100 years ago, they lived in the city of Hull in Humberside. Mr Johnson bought fish from fishermen and sold it to customers.

Mr and Mrs Johnson lived at 154 St George's Road. On 1 July 1903, Mrs Johnson gave birth to a baby girl. The Johnsons named their daughter 'Amy'.

Amy went to school in Hull. When she was 12, she went to Boulevard Secondary School. She was very fond of games and liked going for long cycle rides. She read many books and enjoyed going to the cinema, too.

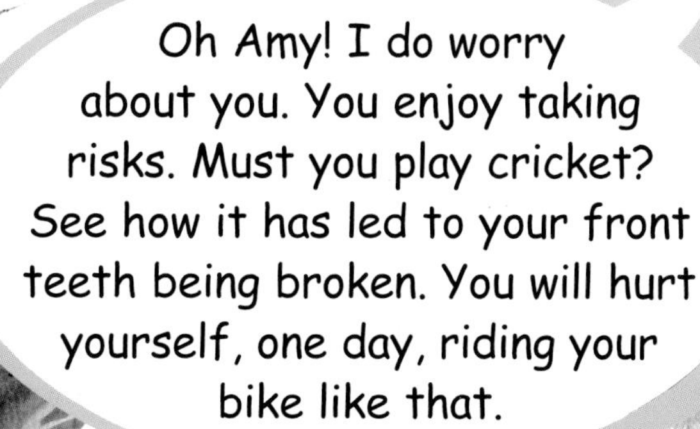

What shall I do?

Many girls became teachers. Amy went to Sheffield University. She enjoyed playing games and going to dances. She was in the university hockey team. Amy got a degree, but she did not want to become a teacher.

Amy's first job was as a secretary. She worked as a typist in Hull, then she moved to London. Amy worked for lawyers there for three pounds a week. This was enough to live on then. She lived in rooms that she shared with her great friend, Winifred Irving.

It is really difficult to know what to do. My friends seem to know what they want to do. I would like to have adventures. My father did, when he was young. He went to Canada to look for gold. What can I do?

Whilst at university, Amy met a young Swiss man called Franz. For several years they met very often. Amy went to Switzerland and met Franz's family. She came to love Franz very much and hoped to marry him. But Franz met someone else. In 1928 Franz married. Amy was still on her own.

In that same year, 1928, Amy visited the London Aeroplane Club. The people there were friendly. Flying aeroplanes looked exciting. Amy longed to find something different to do. Perhaps this was it? So she joined the club and took flying lessons.

Was flying safe?

In 1783, two French brothers made a very big paper balloon. They filled it with hot air. This made it rise high off the ground. Balloons have been flying ever since, though most were soon filled with gas, not hot air.

In 1903, the very year that Amy was born, the first proper aeroplane flew. It was made by two American brothers, Orville and Wilbur Wright. It had a petrol engine and flew for 40 metres.

Six years later, in 1909, an aeroplane managed to fly across the English Channel. Its pilot was a Frenchman called Louis Bleriot. This showed that aeroplanes might become very important.

Between 1914 and 1918 there was a terrible war in Europe. The countries that were fighting used aeroplanes against each other. Aeroplanes became faster and more reliable at this time.

Amy Johnson in her flying outfit.

The war is over, but flying is still risky. Look at all my clothes and my goggles. I really need them. Pilots like me sit in a cockpit that does not have any roof. I get very wet when it rains. If I did not have thick gloves I would get frostbite, it is so cold and windy.

My controls tell me how high I am and how fast I am going. I have a compass to help me find my way. But usually I fly low down and look for buildings and roads and railways to follow.

Learning to fly

The London Aeroplane Club was set up in 1925. Amy had a very happy time there. Flying was becoming popular. Several famous people learned to fly – including some women. Pilots who completed difficult journeys and who did journeys in fast times became very famous. They included an American, Charles Lindbergh. He flew, alone, across the Atlantic Ocean in 1927.

I have got my pilot's licence. It has taken 16 hours of flying with an instructor. Lessons cost £1.50 for an hour, so it is good that my father has been so helpful. Now I can borrow the club's aeroplanes. I love flying, but I must admit that landing is the hardest part.

Amy became a qualified engineer.

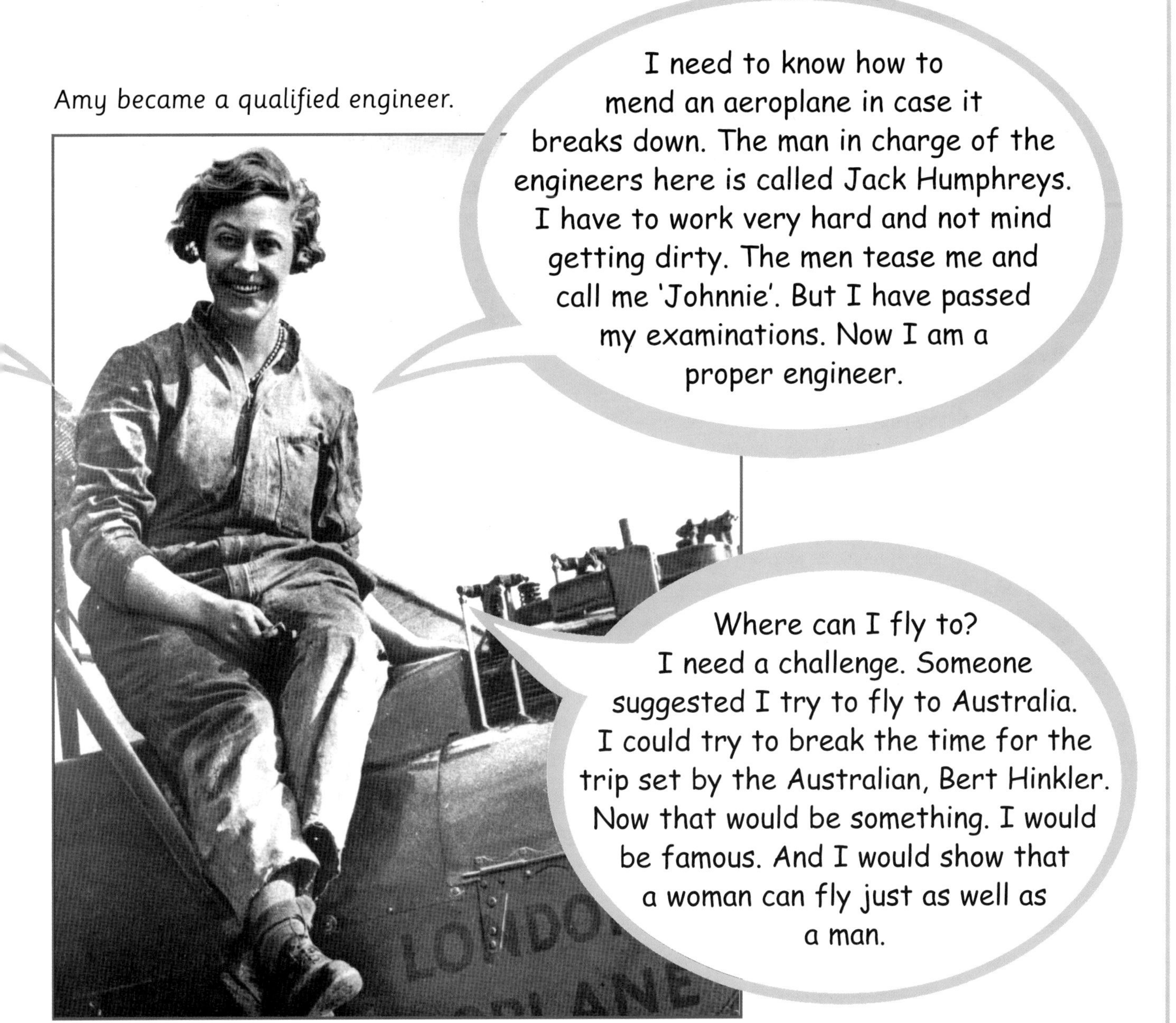

To Australia

THE TIMES

26-YEAR OLD WOMAN TO FLY SOLO TO AUSTRALIA

THE DAILY EXPRESS

WOMAN TO TAKE TO THE SKIES ALONE

Amy needed an aeroplane and all sorts of supplies to fly to Australia. Her father gave her £800 to help her to buy an aeroplane. Lord Wakefield, who was a rich man in charge of an oil company, gave her the rest of the money that she needed. The story of the 26-year-old woman who wanted to fly to Australia got into the newspapers.

Amy's aeroplane Jason.

She bought a two-year-old 'Gypsy Moth' aeroplane and named it 'Jason'. Amy had to plan her journey carefully. It was over 10,000 miles to Australia. She would have to make 22 stops on the way to get more petrol and to rest. Lord Wakefield helped to arrange this. Amy needed maps of all the places over which she planned to fly. She bought a small gun and practised with it. This was in case she had to land in dangerous places.

Amy took off to Australia on 5 May 1930.

Jason flew at a speed of about 100 miles an hour. Amy tied an extra propeller to the aeroplane in case the one that pulled Jason along broke. The wings were made of pieces of wood, with cloth stretched over them.

Amy set off from Croydon airport on 5 May 1930. She meant to leave early, but first a petrol leak needed mending. When she first tried to take off, she failed. At 7:45am she finally took off. Her father, Jack Humphreys and other friends waved her goodbye. Amy had been a qualified pilot for less than a year. She had only ever flown in England. Now she was setting off to fly across the world.

Adventures

The journey to Australia was very difficult. Amy stopped overnight at several places, but usually only had about three hours' sleep, because she was in a hurry. She was trying to fly to Australia faster than anyone had done before. Amy had fruit and sandwiches for her meals, eating as she flew along. She became very sun-burned and dirty. At a few places she was able to have a bath and put on clean clothes.

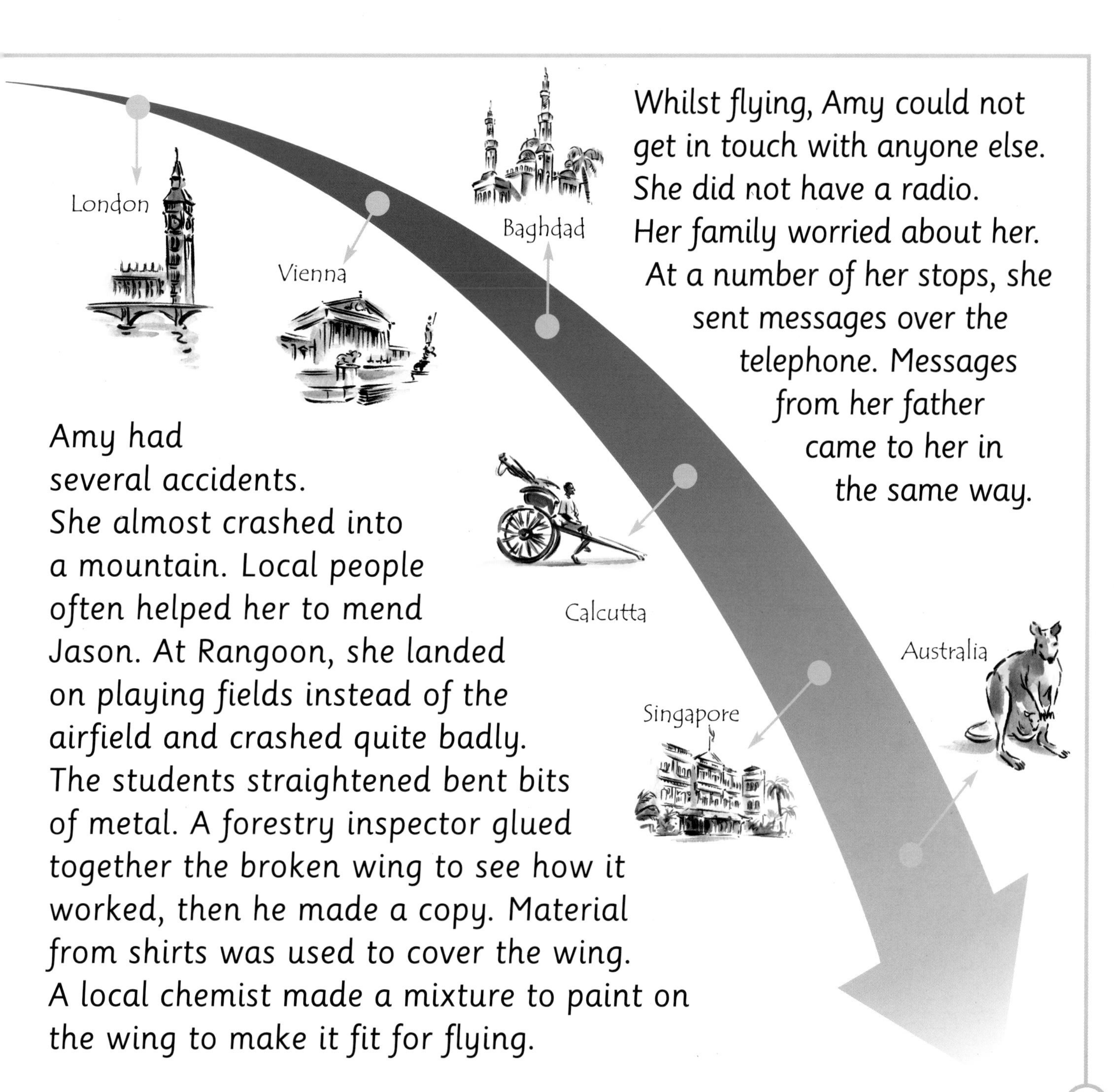

Whilst flying, Amy could not get in touch with anyone else. She did not have a radio. Her family worried about her. At a number of her stops, she sent messages over the telephone. Messages from her father came to her in the same way.

Amy had several accidents. She almost crashed into a mountain. Local people often helped her to mend Jason. At Rangoon, she landed on playing fields instead of the airfield and crashed quite badly. The students straightened bent bits of metal. A forestry inspector glued together the broken wing to see how it worked, then he made a copy. Material from shirts was used to cover the wing. A local chemist made a mixture to paint on the wing to make it fit for flying.

Famous

News of Amy's adventures spread even as she travelled. When she landed in India, on her way to Australia, she found she had completed the journey to there from England faster than anyone else had ever done. Finally, she arrived in Australia – the first woman to have made such a long flight. Her dream had come true. The newspapers were full of stories about her. Lots of people wrote to her to tell her how wonderful she was. The *Daily Mail* newspaper paid her £10,000 for her story. King George V gave her a medal.

Amy was famous when she returned to England.

Crowds gathered to see Amy wherever she went. She met important people. She had to give talks. She went to dinners and dances. After travelling around Australia, Amy returned home. About a million people gathered to see her drive into London. The people of her hometown of Hull made a great fuss of her.

New adventures

Amy looked for new records to break and new journeys to make.

In 1931, she tried to fly across Russia to China, but it was winter and she had to give up. Later that year she flew from Moscow to the city of Tokyo in Japan. For much of the way she followed a railway line to guide her. This railway was called the 'Trans-Siberian'. Her flight took ten days and was a new record.

Amy's next adventure took her to South Africa. She broke the record for this trip, too. There, she met a Scottish pilot called Jim Mollison. When they met again in England they decided to get married. By now aeroplanes were faster and more comfortable. Amy flew an aeroplane called a 'Puss Moth'. It had a cabin in which the pilot was sheltered from wind and rain.

Amy and Jim decided to fly together in a bigger aeroplane. They hoped to win the record for long-distance flying, but they only got as far as America. They ran out of fuel and crashed. Both Amy and Jim were hurt.

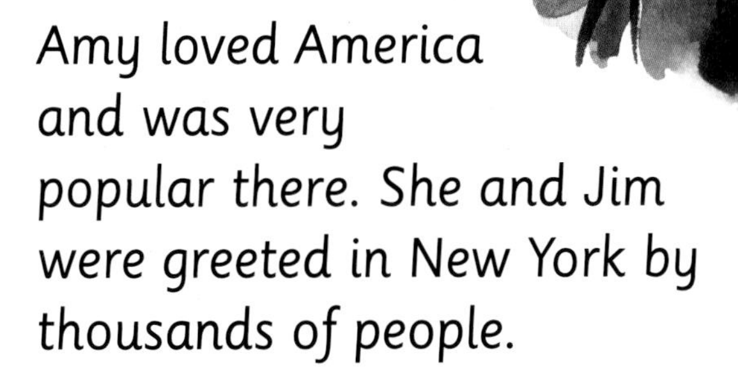

Amy loved America and was very popular there. She and Jim were greeted in New York by thousands of people.

In 1934, Amy and Jim took part in a race by air to Australia. They flew a fast aeroplane called a 'Comet'. They got to India very quickly, setting a new record. But then their aeroplane's engine needed repairs. They had to give up.

Two years later Amy again flew to South Africa. She flew alone and won back her record by beating the time for the flight by 11 hours. Then she flew back in record time, too.

Amy vanishes

By now Amy's marriage to Jim had ended. She lived on her own and spent her time motoring, horse-riding and flying. She earned money by writing.

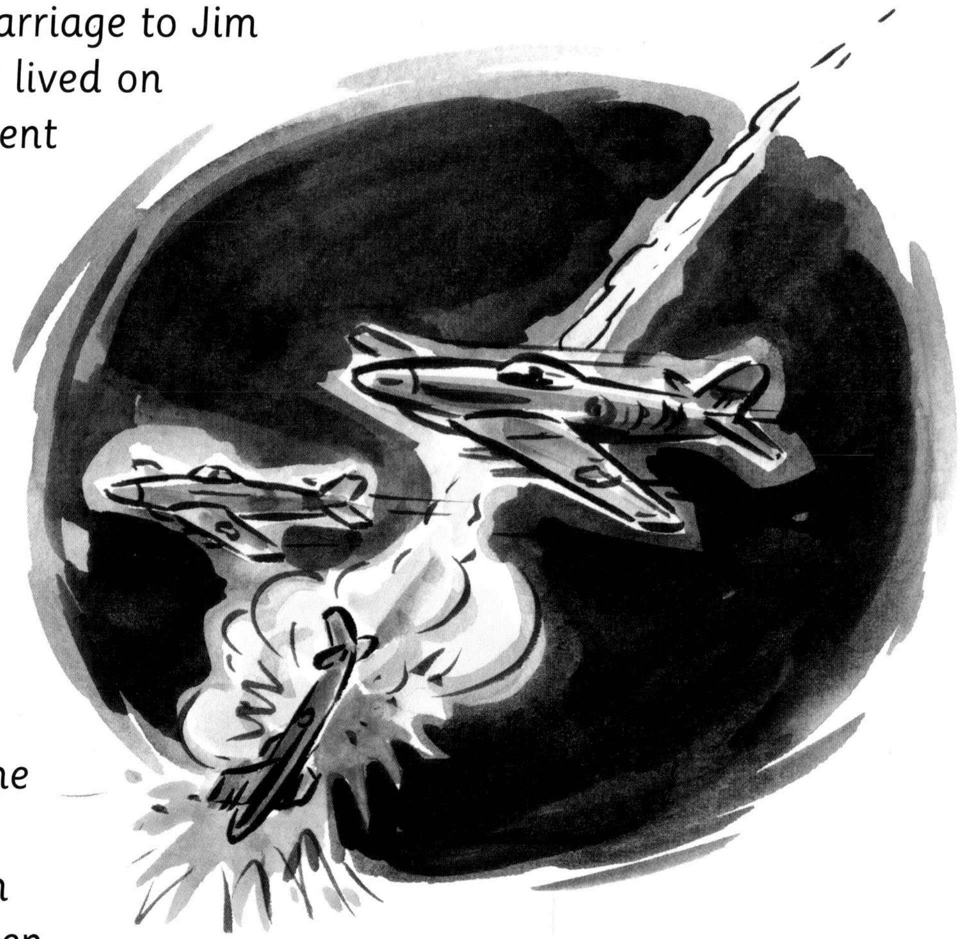

In 1939, a war began between Britain and Germany. Aeroplanes were very important in the war. Each side used them to shoot down their enemies. Women were not allowed to fight in the war. Amy helped the Royal Air Force by flying aeroplanes from the factories where they were made, to the Royal Air Force's airfields.

On 5 January 1941, Amy flew south to deliver an aeroplane. She visited her sister in Blackpool. The weather was not good. Before she left the airfield in Blackpool, one of the pilots there told her it was too risky to fly. But Amy took no notice. She took off 11 minutes before midday and was never seen again.

It is not clear what went wrong. Amy was flying over the River Thames in London in bad weather. She used her parachute and jumped out of the aeroplane. Her aeroplane crashed, but her body was never found.

Amy's family were very proud of her. They filled a room with pictures of her and all the cups and medals that she had won. The gold cup that she gave to Hull can still be seen there. It was made from gold coins collected by children in Australia and is called 'The Amy Johnson Cup – For Courage'. It is still given to a child in Hull every year. One of Hull's schools is called the Amy Johnson School. There is a statue of her in Hull's shopping centre.

Amy's aeroplane, Jason, can be seen in the Science Museum in London. Many books have been written about Amy. Some people can still remember the popular song about her called 'Amy, Wonderful Amy'.

A timeline of Amy's life

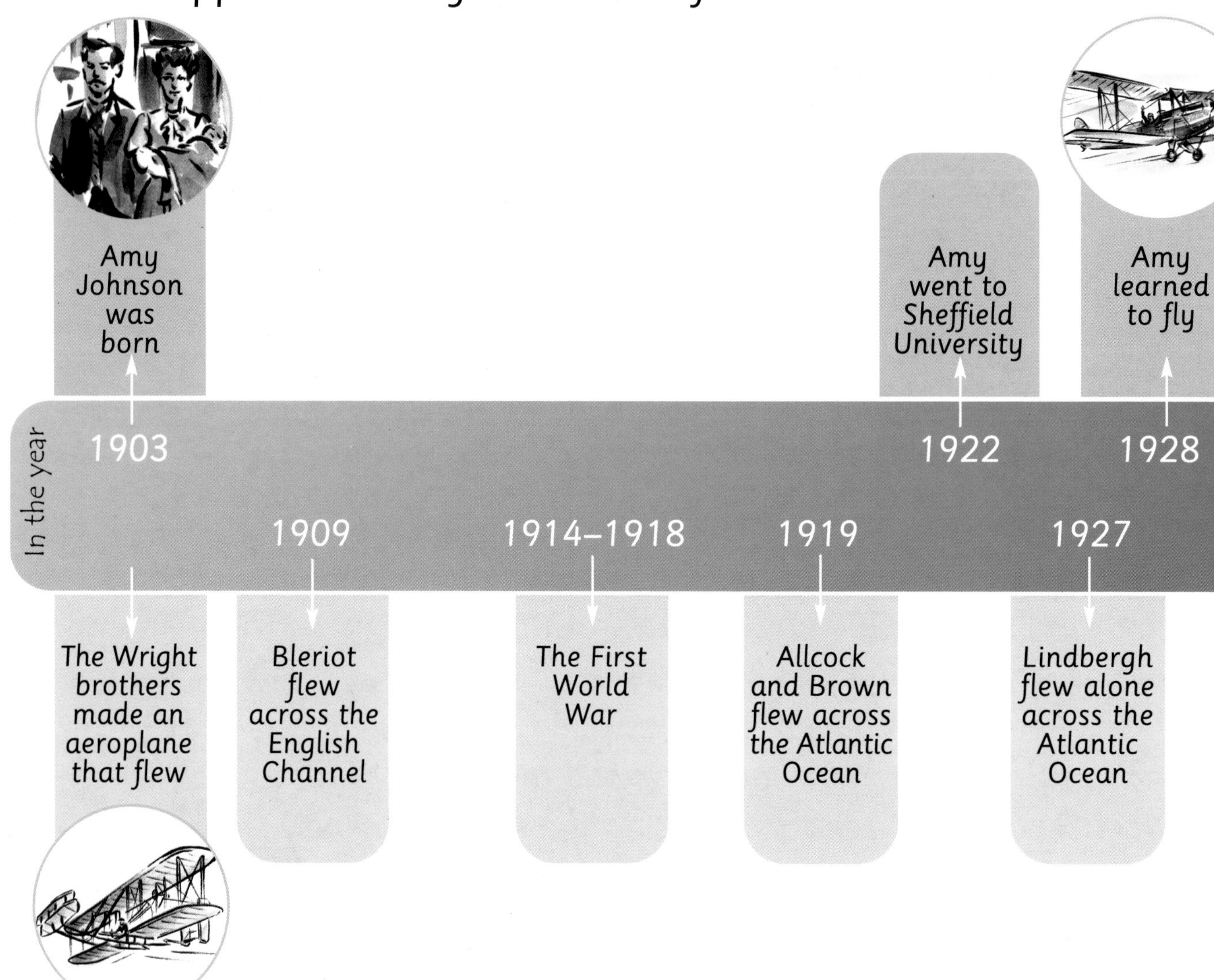

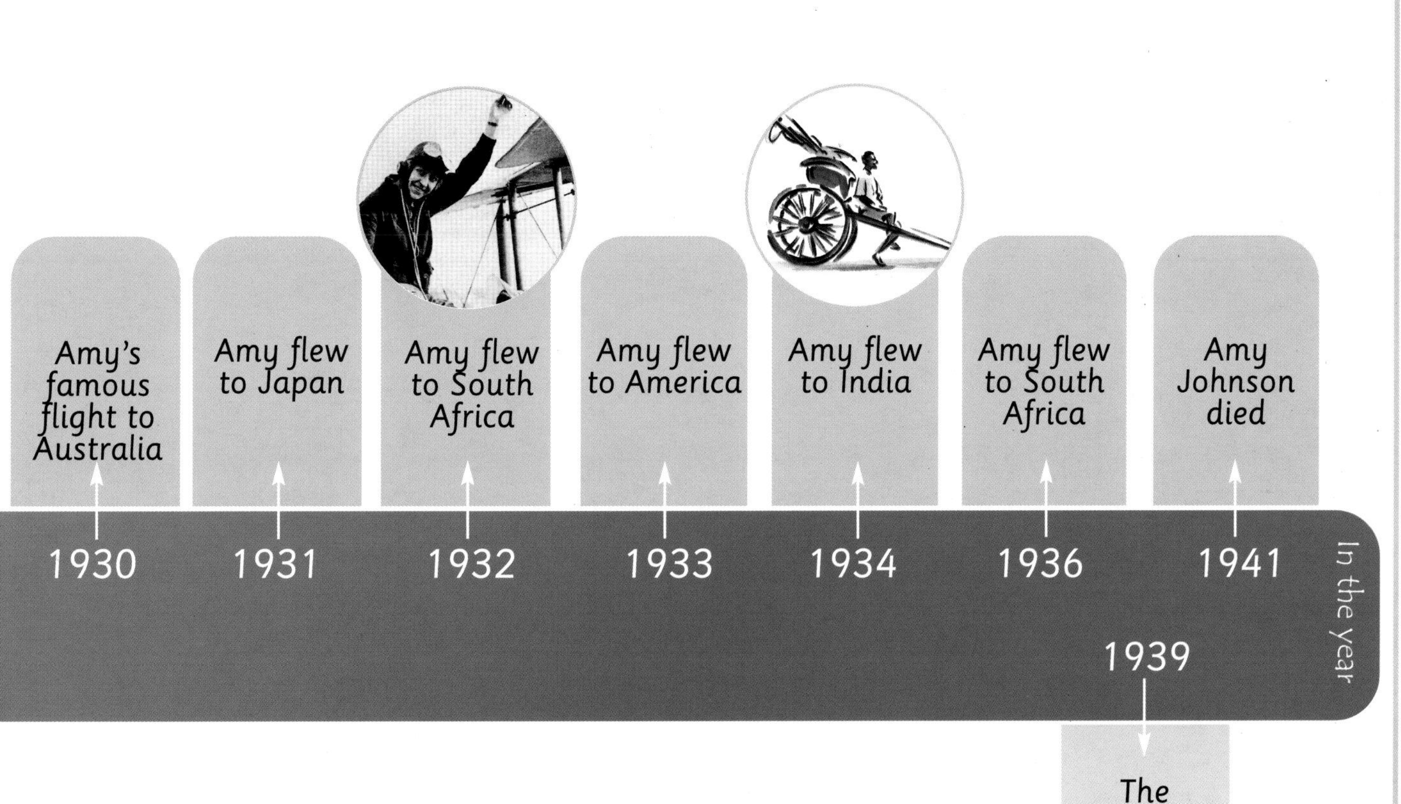
Amy's famous flight to Australia
1930
Amy flew to Japan
1931
Amy flew to South Africa
1932
Amy flew to America
1933
Amy flew to India
1934
Amy flew to South Africa
1936
Amy Johnson died
1941
In the year
1939
The Second World War began

Index

More books to read

Amy Johnson
by Constance Babington-Smith
(Collins, 1967)

Amy Johnson Queen of the Air
by Gordon Snell
(Hodder and Stoughton, 1980)

Silvered Wings
(Hull City Council, 1980)